It's Fun to Learn

I Spy Shapes

One day Roo was playing with a hat Kanga had made out of newspaper.

"Look at me, Mama!" cried Roo. "I'm a pirate!"

"Yes, you are, dear," Kanga replied, smiling.

"Thanks for making me this hat, Mama!" Roo said.

"Roo, dear, do you know what shape your hat is?" Kanga asked.

"My hat is a shape?" Roo asked, removing it from his head so he could get a better look. "Wait, Mama! Let me guess. The shape of my hat is…a triangle!"

"Very good, Roo dear," Kanga replied. "It *is* a triangle."

"And I know why it's a triangle, too," Roo added. "It's because it has three sides!"

"That's right. Can you spot some more shapes?" Kanga asked. "They're all around us."

"You have squares on your apron," Roo said as he followed Kanga inside.
"Yes, dear," said Kanga. "Now it's time to go to Rabbit's garden for more vegetables. I'm afraid I don't have any carrots or tomatoes."

Roo was disappointed. He wanted to stay and play.

Kanga promised Roo that he could play in Rabbit's garden.

"Aw, Mama," said Roo. "You know Rabbit gets fussy when I play in his garden."

"Well, I have an idea that won't bother Rabbit," said Kanga. "Just follow me. Now would you like to hear about the game?"

Roo nodded his head enthusiastically.

"It's called *I Spy*," said Kanga. "I spy something shaped like a circle. Can
you guess what it is? Here's a clue: It rhymes with *tall*."

Roo looked all around him. There were trees and pebbles and...a ball!

"It's that ball!" Roo shouted.

"Very good, Roo!" said Kanga. "Now listen to what else I spy: a diamond flying in the sky!"

"It's Eeyore's kite!" shouted Roo as he bounced up and down excitedly.

"That's right, Roo dear!" Kanga said.

"Hey, this is fun!" Roo said. "Will you give me another riddle? Please?"

"Let me see...," said Kanga. "I spy another circle somewhere nearby."

"Where, Mama?" asked Roo. "Can you give me a clue?"

"It's round and strong and made of wood. It always brings us something good."

Roo looked at Rabbit's garden. First he found some vegetables Rabbit had picked for his supper...and then Roo spotted a circle.

"It's the wheel on Rabbit's wheelbarrow!" he shouted.

"I spy something square, and it's standing over there." Kanga pointed.

Roo was puzzled. What shape was a square again? He couldn't remember.

Just then a bird flew down and landed on a sign near Rabbit's house.

"There it is, Mama! There is the square!" cried Roo. "It's the sign Rabbit put up to tell us he has fresh vegetables."

"How did you know that was a square?" asked Kanga.

"Because it has four sides, and they're all the same length," Roo said excitedly.

"A-tisket, a-tasket, I spy oval shapes in that basket," Kanga said.

Roo quickly looked to the window where Kanga was pointing.

"You mean those eggs are ovals?" he asked.

"That's right, dear," Kanga replied.

"Now I've found a triangle, a circle, a square, and an oval," Roo cried. "This is fun, Mama! What other shapes can we find?"

"Well, there are rectangles," said Kanga. "Spotting a rectangle can be fun. I spy Rabbit holding one."

"It's his carrot sign!" shouted Roo. "That's a rectangle."

Just then Rabbit looked up and saw them arriving.

"Hello, Kanga! Hello, Roo! Are you here for some fresh vegetables?"

Roo bounced over to greet Rabbit.

"Hi, Rabbit!" said Roo. "That's a rectangle you're holding, and it has a carrot painted on it shaped like a triangle."

"Well, yes, I believe you're right," Rabbit said.

"Roo is looking for shapes in your garden," Kanga added.

"I spy lots of shapes," said Roo.

"Hello, Rabbit! Hello, Kanga and Roo!" said Christopher Robin, who had just arrived. "I spy some shapes, too. In fact, I spy an oval that's big and blue. If you guess what it is, I'll give it to you."

"It's your balloon!" cried Roo.

"It's an oval, just like the eggs," Kanga added.

"I spy something, too," Roo said shyly.

"What is it, dear?" Kanga asked.

"Here's a clue to give you a start," Roo said. "My secret shape is a big red heart!"

Kanga looked around Rabbit's garden.

"Hmm," she said. "Where do I see a heart shape?"

"Can you guess, Mama?" Roo asked eagerly. "Can you?"

"It's on Rabbit's garden gate!" said Kanga at last.

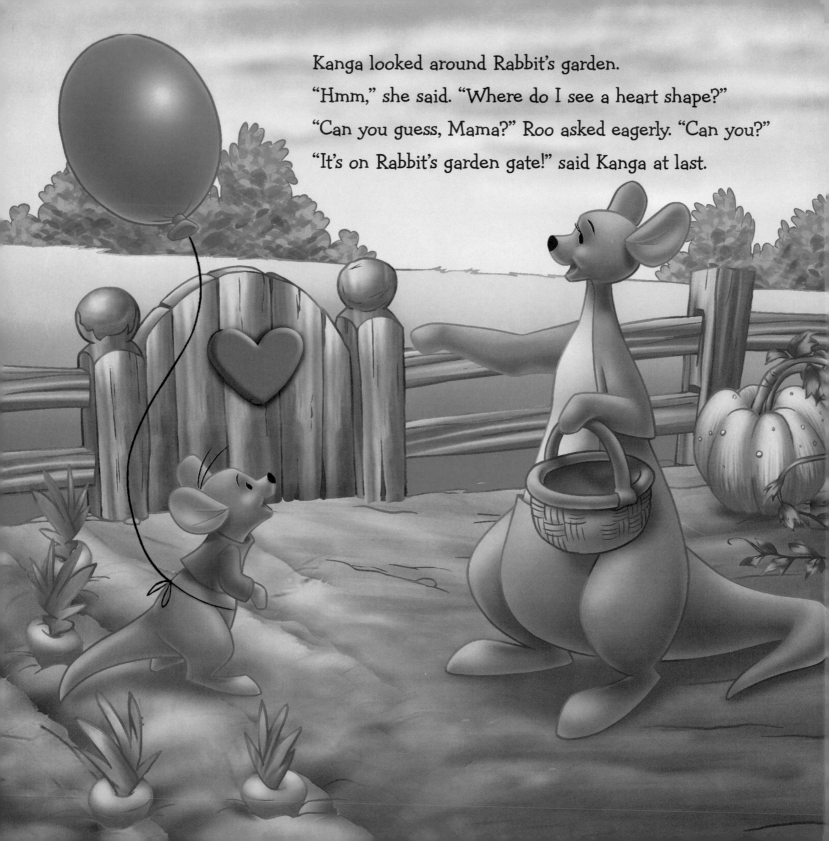

"That was very clever, Roo!" said Christopher Robin.

"Very clever!" cried Rabbit. "Now I have a riddle for you: I spy an oval not far away. It's green, and it's ready to pick today."

Christopher Robin, Kanga, and Roo looked around the garden.

"A watermelon!" yelled Christopher Robin and Roo at the same time as they spotted the oval-shaped fruit on a vine nearby.

"Hooray!" cried Rabbit. "You're right!"

"This game sure is fun, Mama!" Roo said. "Who has another one?"

"I don't spy anything here, but I can think of a rectangle shape," said Kanga. "When we go home down that little path, this shape will be waiting for you in your bath."

"I know!" shouted Roo. "It's a bar of soap! That's shaped like a rectangle."

"Good for you, Roo," said Kanga. "And speaking of your bath…"

"Aw, Mama, do we have to go home already?"

"I'm afraid so, Roo," Kanga replied. "But why don't you take one last look in my basket and see what shapes you can find in there?"

Roo looked at all the vegetables Kanga had picked out. He saw a triangle, an oval, and a circle.

They were the carrots, potatoes, and tomatoes!

"They look yummy, Mama," Roo said. "Maybe it is time to go home. I'm hungry!"

"Wait!" said Rabbit. "Don't go yet!"

"Rabbit, do you have one last riddle for us?" asked Roo.

"I certainly do!" said Rabbit. "I spy something sweet to eat. It's precisely a circle, nice and neat."